EXPLORING NATURE
FANTASTIC PENGUINS

An exciting, fact-filled journey through the frozen world of these flightless birds, with more than 200 pictures

Barbara Taylor
Consultant: Michael Chinery

ARMADILLO

C O N

This edition is published by Armadillo,
an imprint of Anness Publishing Ltd,
Blaby Road, Wigston, Leicestershire LE18 4SE;
info@anness.com

www.annesspublishing.com

Anness Publishing has a picture agency outlet
for images for publishing, promotions or
advertising. For more information, please visit
our website www.practicalpictures.com.

© Anness Publishing Ltd 2013

Publisher: Joanna Lorenz
Managing Editor: Linda Fraser
Editor: Sarah Uttridge
Picture Researcher: Su Alexander
Illustrations by A Durante,
    Milan Illustrations Agency
Designer: Linda Penny
Production Controller: Mai-Ling Collyer

PUBLISHER'S NOTE
Although the advice and information in this
book are believed to be accurate and true at the
time of going to press, neither the authors nor
the publisher can accept any legal responsibility
or liability for any errors or omissions that may
have been made.

Manufacturer: Anness Publishing Ltd,
Blaby Road, Wigston, Leicestershire
LE18 4SE, England
For Product Tracking go to:
www.annesspublishing.com/tracking
Batch: 6794-22518-1127

TENTS

Brush-tails and Crests

There are 17 species, or kinds, of penguin, gathered into six groups called genera. On these two pages, you can find out about two of these genera: the Brush-tailed penguins and the Crested penguins. The Brush-tailed penguins include the Adélie, Gentoo and Chinstrap species, which all have long tail feathers that seem to sweep the ground behind them, like a brush. The Crested penguins include the Rockhopper, Macaroni, Royal, Fjordland crested, Erect-crested and Snares Island species, which all have bright plumes of feathers above their eyes, like long, feathery eyebrows.

▲ TOUGH CUSTOMERS

Adélie penguins average 70cm/28in long and weigh 4kg/9lb. They have a distinctive white ring around each eye. They are among the toughest penguins, breeding on the coast of the Antarctic continent and on the nearby islands. The breeding population of Adélies is around 2.5 million pairs. They are good divers, feeding on fish and krill.

▼ GENTLE GENTOO

Gentoos have large white marks on top of their heads. They are slightly larger than Adélies and Chinstraps, standing up to 90cm/35in tall and weighing 6kg/13lb. Gentoos are timid and prefer to enter the sea from a beach rather than jump from a ledge. They fish deeper than many other species, down to at least 100m/300ft. About 314,000 pairs breed on the Antarctic peninsula and subantarctic islands.

▲ CHATTY CHINSTRAPS

Chinstraps are among the most common penguins. Some 7.5 million pairs breed on the Antarctic peninsula and subantarctic islands in the south Atlantic, such as South Shetland, and South Georgia. On the Antarctic peninsula, they may breed alongside Adélies. Chinstraps are slightly smaller and more aggressive than Adélies, with an ear-splitting call.

Dressed for Dinner

Penguins walk very upright on land because their feet are set so far back on their body. This upright position, together with their coloration, makes them look rather like people in formal evening dress. The white shirt front and black dinner jacket people sometimes wear resembles the black and white feathers of a penguin. Some cartoonists have drawn people as caricatures of penguins. The most famous example is The Penguin, Batman's criminal arch-enemy.

▲ MACARONI PENGUINS

With a length of 71cm/28in and a weight of 5–6kg/11–13lb, the Macaroni penguin is the second-largest Crested penguin, after the very similar-looking Royal penguin. There are over 11 million breeding pairs. They are named after a group of men who introduced Macaroni pasta to England. Called the Macaroni Club, they wore bright feathers in their caps.

▼ TWIN MOHICAN

Named after its stubby, upright crest, the Erect-crested penguin breeds on islands around southern New Zealand. The total population is fairly small, at around 200,000 pairs. With a length of 67cm/26in and weighing 4–5kg/ 9–11lb, they are larger than Snares or Fjordland penguins, but are generally less aggressive.

SURLY ROCKHOPPER ▶

The most aggressive of all penguins, Rockhoppers are named after their habit of bounding over rocks with both feet together. They often jump feet-first into the water, unlike other penguins, which prefer to walk or dive. Rockhoppers are the smallest of the Crested penguins, with red eyes and a drooping yellow crest. The total breeding population of about 3.7 million pairs nests on islands around Antarctica in the Indian and Atlantic Oceans.

Divers and Ringed Penguins

◀ BIG KING

King penguins are the second-largest penguins after the Emperor. They may weigh up to 14kg/31lb. King penguins look rather like Emperor penguins but have a brighter yellow bib. Their bills open wider than those of any other penguin, allowing them to eat bigger prey. During the day, King penguins make deep dives down to depths of 300m/1,000ft. There are more than a million pairs of King penguins breeding on sub-Antarctic and Antarctic Islands.

The penguins on these pages are either Diving or Ringed penguins. The largest Diving penguins are the King and Emperor. They have their own genus, as do the Little penguin and its close relative the White-flippered penguin. The Yellow-eyed penguin of New Zealand is the only member of the third Diving penguin genus. All Ringed penguins belong to one genus. Ringed penguins have ring-shaped bands of black and white on their chest and head. They are also called the warm-weather group, because they live in warmer places than other penguins.

▼ SMALLEST SPECIES

The smallest of all the penguins, the Little penguin is also called the Blue, or Fairy, penguin. They live in southern Australia and New Zealand. They are smaller than many types of duck, weighing just 1–1.8kg/2–4lb.

▲ SHY RARITY

The rarest of all the penguins, the Yellow-eyed penguin breeds on the south-east coast of New Zealand. This penguin is the third tallest, after the Emperor and King penguins. Unlike most other penguins, it is very shy and will not come ashore if people are around.

◄ PORTUGUESE DISCOVERY

The Magellanic penguin was named after the Portuguese explorer Ferdinand Magellan, who was the first to report its existence, in 1519. It is the only Ringed penguin to have two complete black bands across its chest. Magellanic penguins breed from the coast of Argentina, around the tip of South America to southern Chile, as well as on the Falkland Islands. The world population is probably between one and two million birds.

HUMBOLDT PENGUINS ▼

Sometimes called the Peruvian penguin, the Humboldt penguin breeds along the coasts of Chile and Peru, where the cool Humboldt current creates rich fishing grounds. (The Humboldt current was named after the German geographer Alexander von Humboldt.) Humboldt penguins are probably the least studied of all the penguins in the wild, even though they live near people. They are endangered, mostly due to humans interfering, and less than 10,000 are thought to remain.

▼ AFRICAN JACKASS

African penguins are also called Black-footed penguins, because their feet are black, or Jackass penguins, because their call sounds like a jackass or donkey braying. This is the only penguin commonly found in Africa. It lives in cool water currents off the southern African coast. In the last hundred years, numbers of African penguins have gone down from more than one million birds to about 16,000 birds, due to egg collection, pollution and over-fishing.

LIFE IN THE TROPICS ▼

The smallest of the ringed penguins, the Galapagos penguin lives only on the hot Galapagos Islands, off the western coast of South America. Temperatures in the Galapagos may exceed 40°C/104°F, but the penguins survive because of a cool water current that washes past the islands. They spend the day in the water and come on to land at night, when it is cooler.

The World's

Imagine a penguin that weighs no more than a bag of sugar. That is how much the world's smallest penguin, the Little penguin, weighs. Although the Little penguin is small, it is quite fierce and will bite an attacker or fight with its flippers. Little penguins breed in colonies near the shore and stay in their colonies all year round. They nest underground, so total numbers are difficult to count, but there are several hundred thousand birds in Australia. On south-eastern Australia's Phillip Island, Little penguins have been studied since 1967. Half a million tourists visit them every year.

NIGHT BIRDS

The Little penguin goes in and comes out of the sea only under the cover of darkness, perhaps to avoid predators. When it starts getting dark, the penguins gather in large rafts near the shore. Then, at dusk, they come on to land. They spend the night in burrows or other caves. Nesting penguins stay in their burrows all day, too.

BODY BASICS

Unlike most penguins, the Little penguin has no crests or coloration on its head. Its eyes are grey or hazel, and its bill is black. It has a more stooped posture than the other penguin species and often looks as if it is about to tip over.

SWIMMING STYLE

At sea, the Little penguin lies low in the water, often in small groups. When swimming, it comes to the surface to breathe and then dives down again. The Little penguin usually catches prey by diving down to depths of less than 15m. It catches and swallows small fish under the water but brings large fish to the surface, and then swallows them.

Smallest Penguin

ON GUARD
Both parents feed and guard the chicks until they are eight or nine weeks old and ready to go out to sea on their own. The chicks beg for food greedily, often almost knocking over their parents as they clamour noisily for their meal.

UNDERGROUND NESTS
Little penguins nest in burrows, more often than not using natural holes or gaps under rocks, bushes or buildings. They may nest under railway tracks or in caves. If necessary, pairs of penguins dig a shallow burrow together in sandy soil, using their bills and feet. Nests are usually 1–2m/3–6ft apart and lined with plant material and seaweed. Both parents sit on the eggs for 36 days to keep them warm.

FLUFFY CHICKS
Little penguins usually lay one clutch of two eggs every year. The newborn chicks are covered in grey fluffy down, but soon grow a second coat of brown fluffy feathers. They grow rapidly, reaching their adult weight in four to five weeks.

How the Body Works

Beneath a penguin's feathers is a thick layer of fatty blubber, which keeps it warm and stores energy. Energy stores are particularly important to penguins because they have to go for long periods without food while looking after their eggs and chicks, and when moulting their feathers on land. A penguin's bony skeleton supports and protects its internal organs, such as the heart and lungs. The bones are solid and heavy, helping penguins to dive under the water. (Flying birds have hollow bones to reduce their weight.) The bones inside the flipper are wide and flat, to push the water aside as the penguin swims. The breastbone has a strong ridge, to which the powerful flipper muscles are attached.

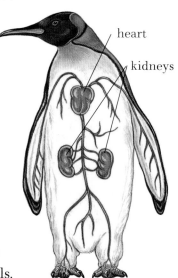

▲ COLD COMFORT

Like all birds, penguins are warm-blooded. They keep their body temperature at a warm 38°C/100°F or so, no matter how cold or hot it is around them. To help them keep warm, penguins rely on their dense, overlapping feathers and a thick layer of fat, or blubber, beneath the skin. Blubber is a bad conductor of heat, so it stops the bird's body heat from leaking out into the air.

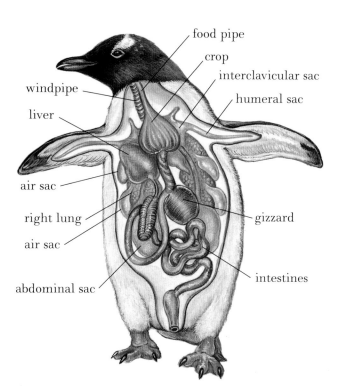

food pipe
crop
interclavicular sac
windpipe
humeral sac
liver
air sac
right lung
gizzard
air sac
abdominal sac
intestines

◀ INSIDE A PENGUIN ▼

These two diagrams show the internal organs of a typical penguin. The one on the left shows the breathing system and the digestive system. The diagram on the right shows the position of the penguin's heart and kidneys, together with some of its blood vessels.

heart
kidneys

HAPPY LANDINGS ▶

Penguins that live in colder places have longer
feathers and thicker blubber than those in
warmer places. Emperor penguins live in the
coldest places of all and are particularly
chubby. Their fatty blubber is useful as a
shock absorber when they leap out of the
sea on to land. It also serves as an energy
store, useful when the Emperors are caring
for their eggs or chicks and cannot get back
to the sea to feed. The large size of Emperors
helps them to stay warm, because they have a
smaller surface area compared to their body
volume than a smaller penguin.

◀ AIR TRAVEL

When penguins swim to and
from their feeding grounds, most
move like dolphins or porpoises,
plunging in and out of the sea.
This is called 'porpoising'. It
allows the penguins to breathe
without stopping and may also
confuse predators. Porpoising
may help penguins to travel
faster, as there is less drag in the
air to hold them back than there
is under the water.

SALTY SOLUTION ▶

Penguins are able to drink sea water
because they have special glands in
their bills that help get rid of extra salt
from the blood. The glands produce a
salty liquid, which is more salty than
sea water and drips out of the nose.
Salty droplets often collect at the tip of
the bill, and the penguins shake them
off, as this Adélie penguin is doing.
Many other seabirds, including gulls,
cormorants, shearwaters and petrels,
also have these salt glands.

Fantastic Feathers

Like all birds, penguins are covered in feathers, but their feathers look very different from those of other birds. Penguins' feathers are small, stiff structures that look more like fur or scales, and are tightly packed above a layer of fine down. This arrangement means that they are smooth and waterproof on top to make swimming easier but warm underneath to stop the penguin getting cold. Penguins preen their own, or each other's, feathers to keep them in good condition. They spend many hours each day preening, especially when they leave the water.

▲ DUVETS AND VESTS

A penguin's feathers are quite stiff and turn over at the tip. They have a fluffy outgrowth near the base, creating a double layer of protection for the skin that is like a fluffy duvet with a string vest on top. The fluffy base of the feathers stops body heat from escaping, while the outer vest stops wind blowing warmth away from the body. If penguins need to cool down, they can ruffle and separate their feathers to allow heat to escape.

◄ WASH AND BRUSH-UP

Penguins must look after their feathers so that they stay waterproof and keep out the cold. To preen its feathers, a penguin spreads oil over them with its bill. The oil comes from a preen gland at the base of the tail. A penguin also uses its bill to tidy its feathers.

▼ YOU SCRATCH MY BACK...

Some species, such as Rockhoppers, preen each other's feathers. This is called allopreening and it occurs between males and females as well as between penguins of the same sex. Allopreening helps penguins to remove parasites, such as ticks, and is important in strengthening pair bonds.

▲ FLUFFY CHICKS

When young penguins hatch, they are covered with warm, downy feathers that make them look very different from the adults. As the chicks grow up, the fluffy down is soon replaced by true feathers.

▼ NEW FEATHERS FOR OLD

While penguins are growing new feathers they have to stay on land and cannot feed. Penguins need lots of energy to grow new feathers so, before they moult, they spend weeks at sea feeding and storing energy in the form of fat. New feathers start to grow under the skin while the penguins are still at sea. After they come ashore to moult, the new feathers push out the old ones.

▲ CHECKING THE RUDDER

On land, penguins use their short, stubby tail feathers to prop themselves upright and help them keep their balance when bending backwards to preen their feathers. Under the water, the short, stubby tail makes a useful rudder to help with steering.

Flightless Wonders

Swift and graceful swimmers and divers, penguins are probably better adapted for life at sea than any other group of birds. They usually travel at speeds of around 7–8kph/4–5mph, using their flippers to 'fly' underwater and their tails and feet for steering, and possibly braking. The small size of penguin flippers helps to reduce drag. On the surface, penguins swim slowly with a small flipper stroke. A large stroke would bring the flipper out of the water and therefore not push the penguin forwards very far. Penguins usually stay underwater for only a few minutes at a time.

▲ DIVING CHAMPIONS

The best penguin divers are also the biggest – Emperor penguins. They can dive to depths of over 400m/1,300ft, although most dives are less than 100m/350ft. The record dive for an Emperor penguin lasted about 18 minutes.

surface

100m/
300ft

Chinstrap
penguin

Little penguin

Gentoo penguin

200m/
600ft

King penguin

300m/
900ft

400m/
1,200ft

Emperor penguin

◄ HOW DEEP DO PENGUINS DIVE?

This chart shows the diving depths of five species of penguin. Larger species can dive to greater depths, because they are able to store greater reserves of oxygen to keep their muscles working. King penguins dive underwater for about seven and a half minutes, while medium-sized penguins dive for three to six minutes. Little penguins rarely dive for more than one minute.

◀ JUST AFLOAT

Penguins' bodies are quite dense – they are heavy for their size – so they float very low in the water. If they were less dense (lighter), they would float higher, but would find it hard to push their way under the water and stay below the surface.
A penguin's darker coloration and markings are only on the top part of the body, partly because this is the part that shows above the surface of the water.

FLIPPER SWIMMING ▶

A penguin's flippers are more like an aircraft's wings than those of birds that fly in air. The long, narrow shape gives a strong propelling action in water, which is much denser than air and needs more effort to push through. The weight of a penguin is countered in water, so the wings just have to propel it forwards.

OUT TO DRY ▼

The flightless cormorants of the Galapagos Islands are the only other sea birds apart from penguins that cannot fly. Their small, ragged wings are too weak for flying or swimming, and they push themselves through the water using their powerful legs and webbed feet. Flightless cormorants hold their wings out to dry their feathers after they have been swimming.

▲ PADDLE STEAMER

Two kinds of South American duck have such short wings that they cannot fly. They are called steamer ducks because of their habit of flapping over the surface of the water with a great deal of spray, like an old-fashioned paddle steamer. These diving ducks use their wings and legs to splash across the surface at speeds of up to 20kph/12mph.

Did you know? When chased by predators, penguins can swim at speeds of up to 12kph/7.5mph.

Waddle, Hop, Slide and Jump

Penguins may look clumsy and awkward on land, but they are actually quite agile. As well as waddling along at about 4–5kph/2.5–3mph, they can leap high out of the water and some can jump over rocks. Uphill, penguins use their flippers to help propel themselves along. On snow, they can slide on their fronts like living toboggans. Some penguins walk long distances to reach their breeding colonies. Emperor penguins travel hundreds of miles over the sea ice to reach their breeding sites. Adélie penguins also make long journeys. They cannot wait for the ice to melt and allow them to swim to their nest sites, because the Antarctic summer is so short and there is little time for breeding. Instead, they walk long distances over the ice and are very good at navigating from the angle and position of the sun.

▼ THE LONG MARCH

Long columns of Emperor penguins march from their feeding grounds out at sea to reach their breeding areas. The side-to-side waddle of a penguin may look awkward, but it helps to save energy, rather like a clock pendulum storing energy at the end of each swing ready for the next swing. Once Emperor penguin parents have chicks, they must travel to and from the sea to catch food for them.

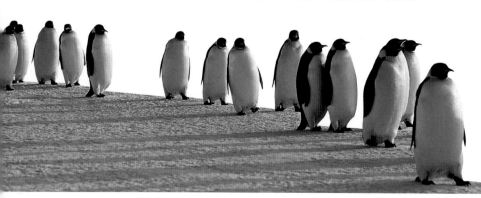

▲ STANDING UP STRAIGHT

When penguins walk on land, they have to stand up straight, with the weight of the body balanced over the feet. This King penguin is stretching up to make itself very tall, probably to display to another penguin. The short, stubby tail of a penguin is not much use for balance but it can be used to prop up its body on land.

Race to the Pole

Members of Captain Scott's expedition to the South Pole struggle to pull a heavy sledge over the ice. In 1910, Scott planned to be the first person to reach the South Pole but found polar travel and survival much more difficult than the penguins. His expedition arrived at the Pole only to find that the Norwegian explorer Roald Amundsen had reached it weeks before them. Tragically, Scott and four companions, Wilson, Bowers, Oates and Evans, all died on the return journey.

▲ ABLE TO BOUNCE BACK

As penguins leap out of rough seas on to hard, sharp rocks or ice shelves, their bodies have to withstand many knocks and bangs. Penguins' squishy blubber helps to cushion the landing but their feathers are also tough and their skin is strong and leathery. This helps the birds to avoid injury as they enter or leave the sea.

◄ LOOK BEFORE YOU LEAP

Rockhoppers get their name from the way they jump from rock to rock with both feet held together. These Crested penguins lean forwards to look at gaps and work out the distance between rocks before they jump. Rockhopper penguins are a bit like human mountaineers, with the ability to climb, bound and claw their way up even steep rocky slopes. Sometimes they use their bill like a third leg to give them a stronger grip on the rock or ice.

TOBOGGAN IN THE SNOW ►

Penguins that live in snowy places often lie down on their chests and slide along. They row themselves along with their flippers and push with their feet or use their feet to act as brakes. In this way, penguins can move faster than they can walk and can travel faster than a person over short distances.

Courtship

Most penguins do not breed until they are two to five years old. Once they have moved to their nest site they display and call to attract a mate. Most keep the same partner for the whole breeding season. Courtship displays are most complex in penguins that nest in large colonies (such as Adélies, Chinstraps, Gentoos and Crested penguins) and less complex in penguins that nest in dense vegetation (Yellow-eyed penguins) or in burrows. In many species, males display first to establish a nest site and attract a mate. This means that the females choose or reject mates, rather than the other way around. A female usually picks her mate from the previous season, unless he fails to return or comes back at a different time.

▲ FEMALE OR MALE?

Female and male penguins usually look alike, and it is difficult to tell them apart. However, in the Crested penguins, such as these Macaronis, the males are larger, more robust and have bigger bills. During the breeding season, female penguins can sometimes be identified by the muddy footprints the males leave on their backs during mating.

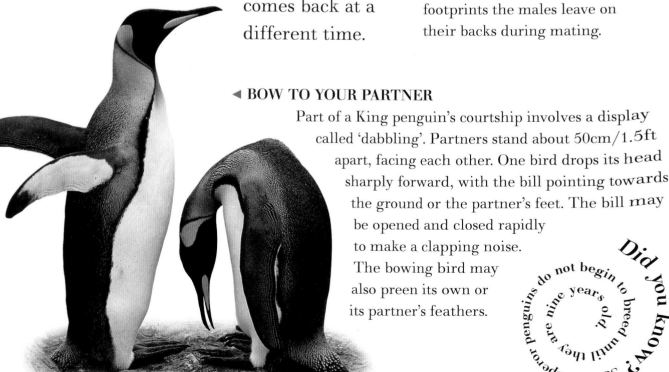

◄ BOW TO YOUR PARTNER

Part of a King penguin's courtship involves a display called 'dabbling'. Partners stand about 50cm/1.5ft apart, facing each other. One bird drops its head sharply forward, with the bill pointing towards the ground or the partner's feet. The bill may be opened and closed rapidly to make a clapping noise. The bowing bird may also preen its own or its partner's feathers.

Did you know? Some Emperor penguins do not begin to breed until they are nine years old.

▼ BALANCING ACT

When penguins mate, the female lies flat on the ground with her flippers out to the side, and the male climbs on her back in a delicate balancing act. Mating lasts for only two or three seconds. If a male tries to mate with a female, and she is unwilling, she stands up and tips him off her back.

▲ AUK COURTSHIP

Little auks display together, both on land and on the water. They also have a special courtship flight, in which the position of the wings and the speed at which they beat are different from normal flying. Eventually, the birds pair up and carry out displays such as the courtship walk, with the male following the female and holding his head down. The auks also face each other and make rapid side-to-side head movements.

▼ CLOSE COUPLE

A pair of King penguins mate about two to three days after they have settled at a particular site. After a long period of a bowing display called 'dabbling', the male either hooks his neck over the female and presses her downwards or leans forward against the female's back. The male may also rub the female's neck with his bill. After mating, a King penguin pair may perform some more dabbling displays.

▲ OSTRICH DANCE

Male ostriches display to females by squatting and waving their huge black and white wings, one after the other. If the brown females are ready to mate, they lower their head and both wings and quiver their wings.

Early Days

Young penguins are quite a different coloration and pattern from the adults. This probably helps to protect them in the colonies, because adults do not see them as competitors for mates or nesting sites. They do not need to be camouflaged from enemies, because they nest in remote areas, usually with large numbers of other penguins around to keep them safe. Duties such as feeding and guarding are usually carried out by both parents equally, except in Crested penguins where the male stands guard and the female brings food for the chick. Parents also spend some time grooming their young, which may distract the young from constantly begging for food.

▲ **SAFE AND WARM**
For the first two to four weeks of their lives, penguin chicks rely on their parents for warmth and protection. Emperor penguin chicks seem especially snug, tucked safely away on the feet of the adults.

◀ **ALWAYS HUNGRY**
By the time they are two or three weeks old, young penguins have grown a thick coat of brown or grey down. They look like giant balls of fluff with big feet and small heads, and quickly become almost as large as their parents. Because of this growth, penguin chicks are always hungry. Their parents have to work very hard catching food in the sea and bringing it back for them to eat.

▼ **SKUA ATTACK**
Young penguins are more at risk from predators than adults, but adults defend their eggs and young fiercely. Predators patrol the colonies on the look out for chicks on their own. If a parent leaves its egg for just a few minutes, predators are always ready to pounce.

▲ MEAL TIME

Newly hatched chicks beg for food by stretching their heads upwards, waving them around and giving shrill, piping calls. Older chicks, such as this one, peck at their parents' bills. The chick pushes its bill into the parent's mouth, and the parent brings up food from its stomach. Chicks of large species may eat over 1kg/2lb at a time.

Batman and the Penguin

Arch-enemy of Batman, the Penguin, has appeared in comics, movies and on television since 1941. His real name is Oswald Cobblepot, and he was born with a short, wobbly body, a bird-like nose and a bad temper. His rich parents dumped their ugly and deformed baby, but he was taken in by a flock of penguins in Gotham City Zoo. In the 1992 film Batman Returns, *Danny De Vito plays the grown-up Penguin.*

▲ LEAVING HOME

When chicks have grown all their feathers, they are said to have fledged. They can then leave the colony to swim in the sea. Parents do not go with their fledged chicks, so the youngsters have to be able to look after themselves. Young penguins stay at sea for the first few years of their life. Penguins may live between 6 and 20 years.

▼ CHANGING CLOTHES

Fluffy down feathers are not waterproof, and chicks cannot go into the water until they have grown their waterproof adult feathers. It takes only seven weeks for Adélie chicks to lose their down, but King penguin chicks may stay fluffy for as long as 13 months. While their adult feathers are pushing through the skin, young penguins, like this Erect-crested, look ragged and untidy.

Where Penguins Live

Penguins live only in the southern half of the world, where cold water currents carry nutrients along the coasts of South America, southern Africa, Australia, New Zealand and the Falkland Islands. Four species – Emperor, Adélie, Gentoo and Chinstrap penguins – breed on the Antarctic continent, but more than half of all penguin species never visit Antarctica at all. The greatest variety of penguins live on the mainland and islands of southern New Zealand and the Falkland Islands.

▲ THE ICE PENGUINS

Emperor penguins are truly the penguins of ice and snow. They live within the ice that floats around Antarctica and usually avoid the open waters beyond it. Sometimes they dive into seal holes or cracks in the ice to feed. Even their breeding colonies are usually on the ice.

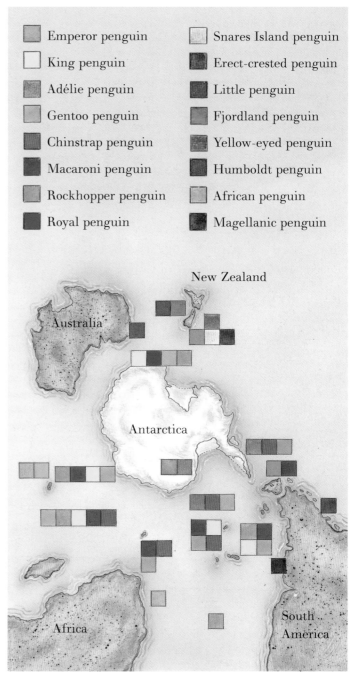

	Emperor penguin		Snares Island penguin
	King penguin		Erect-crested penguin
	Adélie penguin		Little penguin
	Gentoo penguin		Fjordland penguin
	Chinstrap penguin		Yellow-eyed penguin
	Macaroni penguin		Humboldt penguin
	Rockhopper penguin		African penguin
	Royal penguin		Magellanic penguin

New Zealand

Australia

Antarctica

Africa

South America

▲ SOUTH OF THE EQUATOR

Penguins are found on every continent in the Southern Hemisphere and each continent has its own unique species. Penguins may have originally spread from the area around New Zealand, gradually moving south towards Antarctica and north towards the Equator.

◀ A PLACE OF THEIR OWN

Royal penguins are found only on Macquarie Island, which is in the Southern Ocean between New Zealand and Antarctica. Here they nest among the lush tussock grasses, using the same areas every year. Royal penguins are very similar to Macaronis, but have white feathers on their face and throat.

▼ DRY ROCK

Humboldt penguins live along the dry coasts of Peru and Chile. They nest on rocky shores, in sea caves or among boulders. The Humboldt penguin range overlaps that of Magellanic penguins by about 300km/200 miles. Usually, the two species breed in separate colonies.

▲ AT HOME ON THE BEACH

The African, or Jackass, penguin lives only in the coastal waters around southern Africa. It breeds on the mainland and offshore islands, and stays in the same area out of the breeding season. Most African penguins do not go farther than 12km/8 miles from land.

SOME LIKE IT HOT ▼

The Galapagos penguin is a most unusual penguin, breeding on the hot desert islands of the Galapagos. It lives only on these islands and nowhere else in the world. Both adults and young remain at their breeding sites throughout much of the year and do not travel away from the islands.

Warming Up, Cooling Down

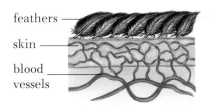

normal temperature – feathers lying down and narrow blood vessels.

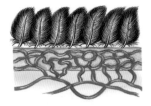

high temperature – feathers ruffled and wide blood vessels near skin surface.

▲ HOT AND COLD

Penguins cannot cool down by sweating. Instead, they open blood vessels near the surface of their flippers, feet and face and ruffle their feathers to let heat escape.

▼ THICK COAT OF FEATHERS

Adélie penguins have to survive temperatures below freezing. They need to stay active in the water to generate body heat, which helps them to keep warm. Adélies have lots of long feathers, which hold a thicker layer of warm air close to the skin than those of other penguins.

From the tropical heat of the Galapagos to the bitter cold of Antarctica, penguins have to work hard to keep their temperature steady. Like all birds, they generate their own heat rather than relying on the sun to warm them up. Fatty blubber and air trapped by a penguin's feathers help to keep warmth in. Penguins can also shiver to create heat, hold their flippers close to their bodies or huddle together for warmth. They can even reclaim about 82 per cent of the heat from the air they breathe out through the nose. Penguins are so good at keeping warm that they sometimes have trouble with overheating. Adélies even seem to suffer from the heat if the temperature gets much above freezing.

▲ COMPLETELY WATERPROOF

A penguin's feathers can be pulled into different positions by small muscles. On land, the feathers are raised to trap a thick layer of air next to the skin, which stops body heat escaping. In water, feathers are flattened to form a watertight barrier, forcing out air.

▼ SHADY CHARACTERS

These Magellanic penguins are huddled in the welcome shade of a bush to stay out of the direct sun. They are holding their flippers away from their bodies so they act as radiators to let heat escape. African elephants use their large ears in a similar way to help them cool down.

▲ BARE SKIN RADIATORS

Penguins that live in warmer places, such as these African penguins, can lose heat from bare patches on the face, flippers and feet. These act as radiators, allowing excess body heat to escape into the air, which cools the penguin down.

▼ COOL BURROW

Magellanic penguins nest in burrows, which gives them somewhere private to escape from the heat. It is much cooler underground than out in the hot sun. These penguins go to sea to catch food during the hottest parts of the day, which also helps them to avoid overheating on land.

COLD FEET ▶

When they are resting on land, Emperor and King penguins tip up their feet and put their whole weight on their heels and tail. This reduces the amount of bare skin in contact with the ice and stops the penguin's feet from getting too cold. The way a penguin's blood circulates inside its feet also helps to retain heat inside the penguin's body. It keeps the penguin's feet at around the same low temperature as its surroundings, so it does not lose too much heat through its feet.

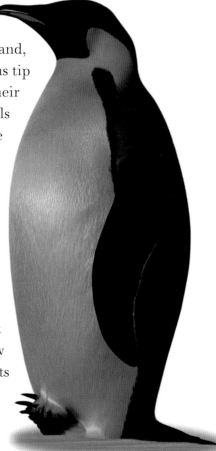

Penguins

The smallest of the Ringed penguins is also the most extraordinary, living only on the Galapagos Islands. These 19 remote islands are on the Equator, 1,000km/700 miles west of Ecuador, in South America. Galapagos penguins breed mainly on the coasts of Fernandina and Isabela Islands, usually feeding at sea during the day and returning to the land in the cool of the night. They sometimes come ashore for short periods during the day. Galapagos penguins often show signs of heat stress when they stand in the sun. When they are really hot, they pant rapidly. As water evaporates from the tongue, it takes heat away and cools the penguin down.

VOLCANIC HABITAT
The Galapagos islands are the remains of volcanoes that rose up from the sea bed millions of years ago. The islands consist of jagged black volcanic rock and dry cactus scrub, a challenging habitat for penguins. They cannot toboggan, as penguins living on smooth ice and snow can. Galapagos penguin colonies are always near the sea; in fact, they are never more than 50m/150ft inland.

OUT IN THE SUN
On land, Galapagos penguins shade their feet with their body to keep them cool. They also hold their flippers out to allow any wind to reach as much of their body as possible and blow any excess heat away from their body. Heat is lost from the undersides of the flippers and the feet, which are not so heavily insulated with fat and feathers as the rest of the body.

from the Galapagos

A COOL DIP

Galapagos penguins can cool off by swimming in the sea, which is always colder than the land. When they swim on the surface, the penguins hold their flippers under the water, which helps them to keep cool. For the same reason, they rarely leap in and out of the water like porpoises, as other penguins do.

HUNTING FOR A MEAL

The Galapagos penguin eats small fish such as sardines. It catches prey by diving but usually stays underwater for less than 30 seconds. There are more fish when the surface waters are cool, and these penguins do not breed unless the water falls below 24°C/75°F.

SIMPLE NEST

Galapagos penguins' nests are usually in shaded places, such as crevices in the rock. They also make simple nest scrapes on the surface, lined with bones, leaves or feathers. The penguins share their habitat with marine iguanas and Sally Lightfoot crabs.

Prehistoric Penguins

Penguins are thought to have evolved more than 65 million years ago from flying birds, perhaps similar to modern diving petrels, which 'fly' underwater. No fossils of anything in-between a flying ancestor and a typical penguin have ever been found. There are very few fossils of penguins that have been found, but over 40 different species of fossil penguin have been discovered so far. This means that penguins were once more varied than they are today. The evolution of seals and small whales about 15 million years ago may have contributed to the extinction of large penguins and many of the small ones.

▲ DID ANCIENT PENGUINS FLY?
The short answer to this question is yes! Some extinct species have features similar to those of modern albatrosses and petrels, both of which can fly. The modern penguin's flipper bones were modified from a flying wing. Its breastbone has areas for anchoring muscles developed originally for flying and its tail bones have a structure which supports tail feathers in all modern flying birds.

▼ EXTINCT RECORD-BREAKERS
Some ancient penguins were much taller and heavier than the Emperor penguin, the largest penguin alive today. The very first fossil penguin to be discovered, *Palaeeudyptes antarcticus* was about 18cm/7in taller than the Emperor. The two largest fossil penguins discovered so far were much larger than this. *Pachydyptes ponderosus* was up to 56cm/22in taller than the Emperor penguin. A fossil penguin even smaller than the Little penguin has also been discovered.

1.8m /6ft

1.8m/6ft human   fossil penguin   largest known living penguin   smallest modern penguin   guillemot   Least auklet

mya = millions of years ago

Present day

Pliocene (5–2 mya)

Miocene (24–5 mya)

Oligocene (37–24 mya)

Eocene (58–37 mya)

Palaeocene (65–58 mya)

Cretaceous (144–65 mya)

Jurassic (208–144 mya)

Archaeopteryx

Ostriches, rheas, cassowaries, emus

Ducks, geese, swans

Pheasants, grouse

Cranes, rails, coots

Auks, waders, skuas

Herons, storks, flamingos

Pelicans, cormorants, gannets, frigate birds

Albatrosses, petrels, shearwaters

Loons, divers

Penguins

Palaeognathae

Anseriformes

Galliformes

Gruimorphae

Charadriiformes

Ciconiiformes

Pelecaniformes

Procellariiformes

Graviidae

Spheniscidae

▲ **CHARTING PENGUIN EVOLUTION**

This chart shows how penguins may have evolved from ancient shearwaters, petrels and albatrosses. Divers and loons probably evolved from the same ancestors but they form a separate group from penguins. Both penguins and divers and loons are more closely related to the shearwaters and petrels, from which they descended directly, than they are to each other.

Living Relatives

Most scientists today think that penguins are most closely related to flying sea birds called tubenoses, which include shearwaters and petrels. Young Little penguins even develop tube-like openings in their nostrils, just like those that adult tubenoses have. Albatrosses, which are also in the tubenose group, have noisy courtship displays similar to those of penguins. Diving petrels 'fly' underwater to chase prey, just as penguins do. When they have moulted their feathers, they cannot fly through the air, but they can still fly very well under the water, like penguins. For the part of the year when they are moulting, diving petrels live very much like penguins, as they are unable to fly. Penguin ancestors probably passed through a stage like this while they were evolving. Apart from petrels and other tubenoses, more distant living relatives of penguins include loons (also called divers), grebes and frigate birds.

▲ **PADDLING PETRELS**
Cape petrels (also called Cape Pigeons or Pintado Petrels) usually feed on the surface of the oceans. They paddle their feet in the water to bring plankton to the surface and peck from side to side. Cape petrels also dive for fish and squid, both from the surface and from the air.

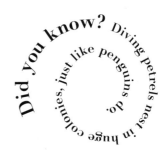

Did you know? Diving petrels nest in huge colonies, just like penguins do.

A LIFE ON THE OCEAN WAVES ▶

Shearwaters glide over the sea on long wings but also dive to catch fish and squid. They use their wings to push themselves underwater and are well adapted for fast swimming. They have strong, streamlined legs, large webbed feet, and compact feathers that enable them to sink more easily. Many shearwaters feed in dim light or at night, like some penguins do. Some fossil penguin bones show features that are very similar to those of shearwaters.

▲ COURTING GREBES

Both grebes and penguins may use nest material in their courtship displays. The weed ceremony of these great crested grebes is part of a complex sequence of displays. Grebes are well adapted to underwater hunting. A diving grebe can move at about 2m/6ft a second and turn very quickly.

▼ IN ITS ELEMENT

After penguins, loons or divers are the most specialized diving birds. They are so well adapted for swimming and diving that they cannot walk properly on land. Unlike penguins, loons use their feet, rather than their wings, to push themselves through the water. They usually hunt fish within 10m/30ft of the surface. Loon chicks can dive just a day after hatching.

▲ SUPER SWIMMER

Seals are not related to penguins – they are mammals, whereas penguins are birds. But seals are a similar shape to penguins because they too are adapted for swimming fast underwater. Seals and penguins both have streamlined, torpedo-shaped bodies. Sea lions even use their front flippers for swimming, although true seals, such as this crab-eater seal, use their back flippers.

▼ AERIAL PIRATE

This male frigate bird has puffed out his throat like a red balloon in order to attract a mate. In the air, frigate birds are agile and acrobatic fliers, plucking fish or squid from near the surface. As well as catching their own food, these large birds steal the prey of others. They chase seabirds and dive-bomb them to force them to drop what they have caught. Frigate birds are such good fliers that they can even grab the falling fish from the air.

Speedy Sprinters

The best known flightless birds, apart from penguins, are ostriches, emus, rheas and cassowaries. These are all big birds with long legs, which can run fast over the ground. They do not need to fly to escape danger, because they can run away instead. They all have large, powerful feet to push themselves along. They also use their feet as weapons to defend themselves. Cassowaries, rheas and emus are also strong swimmers. Even though they cannot fly, these birds do have wings. They may use their wings to help them cool down on hot days, or display them during courtship. Male ostriches, emus, rheas and cassowaries all play an important role in raising the young.

▲ LEGGING IT
The ostrich is the biggest bird in the world. It is much too heavy to fly, but it is a brilliant runner. Ostriches can sprint at speeds of up to 70kph/45mph – that is as fast as a car. At high speed, both feet come off the ground at once.

▲ RESPONSIBLE FATHER
South American rheas can sprint faster than a horse. They are smaller than ostriches and have three toes on each foot, instead of just two. Male rheas build the nest and look after the eggs and chicks. They may incubate up to 60 eggs at once. Females lay their eggs in the nests of several different males.

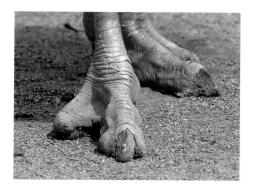

▲ HOW MANY TOES?
Ostriches have just two toes on each foot; most other birds have at least three. An ostrich's toes are strong and end in thick curved claws. They help the ostrich grip the ground as it runs and are also useful for kicking predators, such as lions.

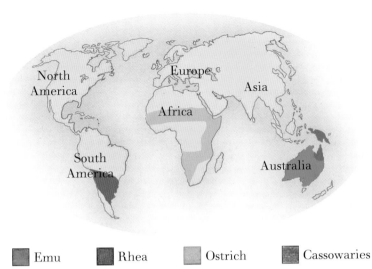

Emu   Rhea   Ostrich   Cassowaries

▲ SEPARATE HOMELANDS

Ostriches, emus and rheas live in different continents. Rheas live only in South America, ostriches in Africa and emus in Australia. They have all adapted to similar habitats and may share ancestors that lived together when all the continents in the Southern Hemisphere were joined together about 150 million years ago.

▲ PROTECTIVE PARENT

The male emu does all the work when it comes to looking after the eggs and chicks. At eight weeks the eggs hatch and the male becomes very aggressive, attacking anything that comes too close.

Feather Headdress

The people of Papua New Guinea keep all three species of cassowary in captivity and often treat them as pets. They pluck the feathers to use in ceremonial headdresses like this one. Some also use the feather quills for nose decoration. The feathers are part of costumes worn on special occasions concerned with the religious beliefs of the people. Dances are performed to respect the spirits of the ancestors. Cassowaries have been traded by people throughout far south-eastern Asia for over 500 years.

▲ BIG BIRD

Cassowaries can be the same height and weight as a person. They live in the rainforests of Papua New Guinea and Australia. The cassowary's long, hair-like feathers help to protect its body and stop its skin getting scratched. Its powerful legs end in dagger-like claws. These birds will even attack people if they feel threatened.

New Zealand's Flightless Birds

The world's most unusual collection of flightless birds live on the islands of New Zealand, about 1,600km/ 1,000 miles south-east of Australia. These birds include the unique kiwi, which is related to the ostrich, emu, rhea and cassowary. New Zealand's other flightless birds are versions of birds that can fly, in other places. These birds gave up flying in New Zealand because there were no land predators to fly away from. Unfortunately, people have introduced mammal predators, such as stoats, to New Zealand. These predators find it very easy to catch the flightless birds and eat their eggs and chicks. Numbers have declined dramatically, and many of the birds are now rare.

▲ SNIFFING OUT A MEAL

Kiwis behave more like furry mammals than birds. Even their thick, shaggy feathers look furry. They help to protect the chicken-sized birds from thorny bushes in the forest. Kiwis come out at night and sniff out food with sensitive nostrils at the tip of their long, curved bill. It is rare for a bird to have such a good sense of smell. Although their eyes are small for a nocturnal creature, kiwis can see well enough to run fast through dense undergrowth at night.

GROUNDED ▶

The kakapo is the world's largest parrot and the only one that cannot fly. It has a thick layer of insulating fat under its skin, which makes up about 40 per cent of its body weight, and is too heavy to get airborne. Kakapos live on the ground and come out at night. Their green feathers help to camouflage them among the ferns and other forest plants. Kakapos evolved at a time when there were no ground predators in New Zealand to attack them or eat their eggs, so there was no need to fly.

▲ FLIGHTLESS PHOENIX

A century ago, people thought that the takahe, a large flightless rail, was extinct. But in 1948, it was rediscovered living in remote alpine grassland in the south-west of New Zealand's South Island. Its story is a bit like that of the mythical phoenix, which catches fire and disappears, only to come alive again from the ashes.

▲ MIXED BLESSING

The weka uses its wings to help keep its balance as it walks. Wekas are large, flightless rails, with powerful feet and strong claws. They have a varied diet, from grass, seeds and fruit, to mice, birds, eggs and beetles. Wekas can be fierce predators of other ground-living birds and have caused serious problems on some islands to which they have been introduced. However, they are very good at killing rats that attack other flightless birds.

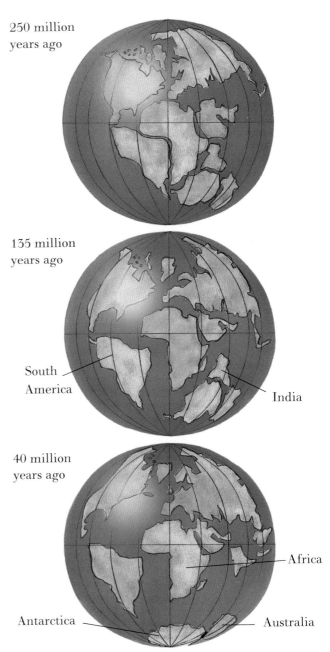

250 million years ago

135 million years ago

South America

India

40 million years ago

Africa

Antarctica

Australia

▲ DRIFTING APART

The islands now called New Zealand were once part of a supercontinent called Gondwanaland, which also included South America, Africa, India, Australia and Antarctica. Gondwanaland began breaking up 180–140 million years ago. Australia and New Zealand separated from Antarctica and moved away around 100 million years ago. New Zealand finally drifted away from the east coast of Australia about 80 million years ago and has been isolated since.

Threats to Penguins

The greatest danger to penguins comes from people. People have polluted the oceans where penguins swim, not only with oil, but also with plastic waste that can trap and kill penguins. People have also destroyed the natural habitat of some penguins on land and over-fished the seas where penguins feed. Humboldt penguins are accidentally killed in fishermen's nets. In some places, predators introduced by people, such as cats, rats and ferrets, eat penguin eggs and chicks. In the past, people gathered penguin eggs to eat and killed the adult birds for their meat, skins, feathers and the oil in their fatty blubber.

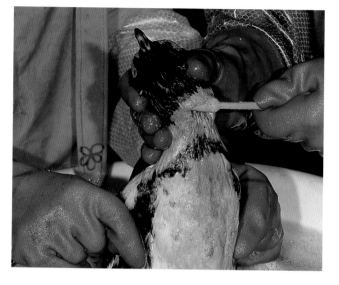

▲ COMING CLEAN

Oil spills from tankers and boats cleaning out their engines at sea have a disastrous effect on penguins. The oil mats their feathers, allowing water to get in. Without a layer of warm air near the skin, penguins die of cold. If they do reach the shore, the oiled birds try to preen their feathers and end up swallowing some of the poisonous oil. This oiled Jackass penguin is being washed carefully after an oil spill off South Africa.

DUG INTO DUNG ▶

Over 2,000 years ago, the Incas of South America used penguin droppings to make the soil rich and help them grow their crops. The Inca word for this naturally dried fertilizer is 'guano'. The Incas were careful to harvest it at a slower rate than the birds produced it, so the supply did not run out. The guano was up to 50m/150ft deep in places. Nowadays, the Humboldt penguin is threatened by over-harvesting of guano. There is not enough left in which these penguins can dig their nesting burrows. Similar damage in South Africa has been recognized and action taken to stop any further deterioration of habitat.

◀ PRESSURE FROM PEOPLE

Many people want to see penguins close up, but if this is not properly controlled, it can seriously disturb the birds and cause their numbers to drop. Low-flying helicopters cause great distress to penguins. Parents may even flee from the nest, exposing eggs and chicks to predators. Disturbance drains a parent's energy reserves, which are already low as a result of nesting or moulting. Stressed penguins cannot look after and feed their chicks properly, and many chicks die.

DWINDLING FOOD SUPPLY ▶

These shrimp-like creatures are krill, an important food item in the diet of many penguins. The amount of krill in the sea is affected by the temperature of the water and the amount of ultraviolet radiation from the Sun. Changes in these two factors caused by pollution have already cut down the amount of plant plankton, which the krill eat. If there is less krill, then penguins starve.

Did you know? In June 1994, around 40,000 penguins were affected by an oil spill off South Africa.

▼ HEAVY HOOVES

This sheep grazing peacefully among Gentoo penguins does not look as if it is causing any damage. However, sheep are heavy animals and they trample penguin burrows and nests as they walk about. Other introduced animals, such as dogs, cats and weasels, are predators that attack the penguins directly.

▲ PENGUINS ON THE MENU

Early European expeditions to the Antarctic, such as Captain Cook's expedition (above), slaughtered penguins for their fresh meat. The trusting penguins were easy to kill. Yet this only had a small effect on penguin numbers. Killing penguins for their oil in later decades devastated many colonies, since it took eight penguins to produce just one gallon of oil.

The Timid

Yellow-eyed penguins breed only around the south-east coast of New Zealand and on the nearby islands of Stewart, Campbell and Aukland. Adults stay on or near their breeding grounds all year round. These beautiful penguins are endangered on the mainland and rare elsewhere. In the last 40 years, their numbers have fallen by at least 75 per cent in some areas. The main reason for this drastic decline is that the forests where the penguins nest have been turned into farms or their trees cut down for timber. More recently, introduced predators, such as cats, pigs, stoats and ferrets, have begun taking chicks. In some areas, all the chicks may be killed within four weeks of hatching.

WHERE TO NEST?

Now that so much of the coastal forest has been cleared, Yellow-eyed penguins are forced to nest in gullies or on hills, cliff tops or slopes that face the sea. These nest sites offer no shelter from the hot sun. Yellow-eyed penguins suffer greatly from heat stress, especially during the breeding season. When they are not looking after chicks, they sleep on land in the cool of the night and go to sea by day.

MUSICAL COURTSHIP

This pair of Yellow-eyed penguins are preening each other as part of their courtship display. It helps to keep the pair together by strengthening the bond between them. Yellow-eyed penguins also court with calls. The loud calls of this species are much more musical than the harsh cries of most penguins.

Yellow-eyeds

PRIVATE HIDEAWAY

Yellow-eyed penguin nests are usually well hidden in dense vegetation and scattered over a wide area. They cannot usually see their fellow penguins, but they can hear them. Both parents build the nest, which is a shallow bowl on the surface made of twigs, grass, leaves and other vegetation.

CAUGHT BY ACCIDENT

Fishing nets can cause problems for Yellow-eyed penguins. They become tangled up in the nets and drown because they cannot swim up to the surface to breathe. Yellow-eyed penguins seem to be most at risk from nets used for catching bottom-living fish. These nets are set in water 100–200m/300–700ft deep.

FOREST NURSERY

The natural breeding habitat of the Yellow-eyed penguin is the cool forests along the coast of south-east South Island, New Zealand, and the islands nearby. In the last 140 years, the coastal forests of the mainland have been almost totally destroyed and replaced by farmland.

NESTING BOXES

Conservation groups such as the Yellow-eyed Penguin Trust are working hard to protect Yellow-eyed penguins. They have bought several areas of the penguin's habitat and are replanting them to provide suitable nesting areas. While the conservation groups wait for the plants to grow, large nest boxes placed in suitable areas encourage more penguins to nest, by providing shelter and protection from the heat of the sun.

Protecting Penguins

▲ HABITAT PROTECTION

Penguin nesting areas were first protected in the early 1900s. In 1919, the penguin oil factories on the Macquarie Islands were closed, and the islands were turned into a penguin sanctuary. These tourists are watching penguins on the Macquarie Islands. In 1961 the Antarctic Treaty agreed to protect all penguins, so they could no longer be legally hunted.

Penguins are enchanting birds. They have done nothing to harm us, yet we have put many of them at risk. One of the problems about penguin conservation is that we know so little about penguins, especially what happens to them while they are at sea. New technology, such as tracking by satellite, is helping to fill in some of the gaps, but there are still many mysteries to unravel. Penguin habitats on land need to be protected and their breeding colonies kept free of unnecessary disturbance. Captive breeding of rare penguins in zoos and wildlife parks may help these species survive in the future. Cutting back on pollution would help those in the wild.

FINDING OUT MORE ▶

To help penguins in the future, we need to find out more about how they live. It is difficult to carry out this research without disturbing the penguins, but researchers try to upset them as little as possible. This researcher is collecting data from a Little penguin chick on Kangaroo Island, South Australia. Penguins are weighed and measured, and their eggs and chicks are counted. The penguins' diet is investigated by flushing out their stomachs with water, and the way in which they behave is carefully observed and recorded. Satellite transmitters are fitted to some penguins to help scientists find out where they go and how far they travel during their time at sea.

60

▲ POPULAR ATTRACTIONS

Penguins did not find their way into most zoos until the 19th century, but they are now very popular exhibits. Penguins in zoos help the public to appreciate how beautiful and interesting live penguins are. They are difficult to transport, and it is expensive to create a cold environment that is close to their natural habitat.

▼ KEEPING A SAFE DISTANCE

Wild penguins are major tourist attractions in New Zealand, southern Australia, South America and Antarctica. In Antarctica, tourist numbers increased from fewer than 300 people a year in the 1950s to more than 5,500 people per year in the early 1990s. At Punta Tombo in Argentina, tourism increased from several dozen people per year in the 1960s to more than 50,000 per year in the 1990s. Tourists need to be aware of how to behave near penguins so that disturbance can be kept to a minimum.

▲ ILLEGAL PRACTICE

In some places people have collected penguins' eggs for hundreds of years. In 1897, more than 700,000 African penguin eggs were taken from colonies off the coast of South Africa. Penguin egg collecting was banned in 1969, but in parts of South America illegal harvesting still continues.

▼ HOLE IN THE SKY

Far up in the atmosphere, 15–90km/10–50 miles above the Earth's surface, is a layer of a gas called 'ozone'. Ozone stops harmful ultraviolet rays from reaching the Earth from the Sun. However, chemicals such as CFCs have caused holes in the ozone layer. The extra ultraviolet radiation coming through the holes damages or kills off the microscopic sea creatures on which fish and penguins feed.

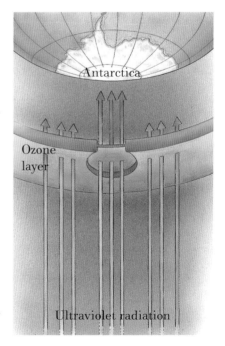

Antarctica

Ozone layer

Ultraviolet radiation

GLOSSARY

allopreening
Preening of one bird by another.

baleen
Horny plates that hang down from the top jaw in some whales and are used to filter food from the water.

binocular vision
Type of vision in which both eyes look to the front and have overlapping fields of view.

blubber
The thick layers of fat found under the skin of penguins and sea mammals, such as whales and seals.

breeding season
The time of year when pairs of animals come together to mate and raise a family.

brood patch
A featherless area of thickened skin underneath a bird's body, used to keep eggs warm during incubation.

camouflage
Coloration, patterns or shapes that allow an animal to blend in with its surroundings in order to hide from prey or escape danger.

carnivore
An animal that eats meat.

clutch
The set of eggs laid and incubated together.

colony
A large number of birds that gather together to breed.

conservation
Protecting living things and helping them to survive in the future.

countershading
The coloration of an animal with a dark back and a light underside, which provides camouflage.

courtship
Ritual displays that take place before mating.

crèche
A group of young in the nesting area, which are still dependent on their parents.

down
Fine, fluffy feathers which help to trap air and keep a bird warm. Young chicks only have down.

drag
The resistance to movement in water or air.

ecstatic display
A 'stretch up and shout' display, usually given by males during the breeding season. It helps to attract females, drive off rivals and lay claim to a nest site.

egg tooth
A small, sharp point on the tip of a baby penguin's bill, which helps it to break free from its eggshell.

endangered species
A species that is likely to die out in the near future.

evolution
The process by which living things change gradually over many generations.

fast
A period of time without food.

flightless
Unable to fly.

flipper
A limb that has been adapted for swimming.

fossils
The preserved remains of animals and plants, usually found in rocks.

genus (plural: genera)
A group of closely related species, such as the Crested penguins.

habitat
The kind of surroundings in which an animal usually lives.

incubation
Sitting on eggs to keep them warm.

insulation
Keeping warm things warm and cool things cool.

iris
A thin disc with a hole (the pupil) in the middle. This is on the front of the lens in the eyes of animals with backbones.

keel
A ridge along the breastbone of birds, supporting the powerful flight muscles or swimming muscles. The larger flightless birds do not have this keel.

krill
Small, shrimp-like sea creatures that swim in huge shoals.

mammal
An animal with fur or hair and a backbone, that can control its own body temperature. Females feed their young on milk made in mammary glands.

moulting
The shedding of old and damaged feathers and the growth of new ones, usually once a year.

mutual display
Interaction between two penguins, usually when they meet at the nest.

navigating
Finding the way to a particular place and following a course.

nictitating membrane
A third eyelid that can be passed over the eye to keep it clean or shield it.

nocturnal
Active at night.

plankton
Tiny creatures that drift with the water movement in the sea or in lakes.

plumage
The covering of feathers on a bird's body.

porpoising
Leaping in and out of the sea's surface, like a dolphin or porpoise.

predator
An animal that catches and kills other animals for food.

preening
The method by which birds care for their feathers, using the bill and oil from the preen gland.

prey
An animal that is hunted and eaten by other animals.

ratites
A group of large, flightless birds, including ostriches, emus, rheas and cassowaries. Although the ratites belong to different families, they have similar features, such as powerful legs, small wings and no keel on the breastbone.

regurgitate
To cough up food that has already been swallowed, to feed chicks.

rookery
A large group, or colony, of animals breeding in one place. Used sometimes for penguin colonies but also refers to groups of rooks (European birds).

species
A group of animals that share similar characteristics and can breed together to produce fertile young.

streamlined
A smooth, slim shape that cuts through the air or water easily.

subspecies
A species is sometimes divided into even smaller groups called subspecies, which may differ in appearance and live in different areas, although they can still interbreed if they meet.

tobogganing
When a penguin slides on its belly, sometimes pushing itself along with its flippers and feet.

INDEX